MARYLAND
The Old Line State

★

TEN TOP FACTS ABOUT MARYLAND

★ ★ ★ ★ ★ ★ ★ ★ ★ ★ ★ ★ ★

•State nicknames:	The Old Line State, America in Miniature, The Free State
•State motto:	*Fatti Maschii, Parole Femine* (Manly Deeds, Womanly Words)
•Capital:	Annapolis
•Area:	10,455 square miles
•State flower:	Black-eyed Susan
•State tree:	White oak
•State bird:	Baltimore oriole
•State insect:	Baltimore checkerspot butterfly
•State crustacean:	Maryland blue crab
•State sport:	Jousting

Photo credits:

p. 4: U.S. Mint; p. 5: (both) North Wind Picture Archives, Alfred, ME; p. 6: (top) Bettmann/Corbis, New York, NY (bottom left) Brown Brothers, Sterling, PA (bottom right) North Wind Picture Archives; p. 7: (both) North Wind Picture Archives; p. 8: (top left) The Granger Collection, New York, NY (top right) Brown Brothers; p. 9: Brown Brothers; p. 10: Bettmann/Corbis; p. 11: Bettmann/Corbis; p. 12: (top left) Bettmann/Corbis, (center) Corbis; p. 13: (top) Superstock Images, Jacksonville, FL (bottom left and right) North Wind Picture Archives; p. 14: (both) North Wind Picture Archives; p. 15: (top) North Wind Picture Archives, (bottom) Monocacy National Battlefield, Frederick, MD; p. 16: (both) Corbis; p. 17: Superstock Images; p. 18: (left) North Wind Picture Archives, (bottom) Corbis; p.19: M. Evans/Maryland Office of Tourism Development; p. 20: (top left) M. Evans/Maryland Office of Tourism Development, (lower left) B. McAllen/Maryland Office of Tourism Development, (right) Kim Hairston, *The Baltimore Sun*, Baltimore, MD; p. 21: (top left) Banneker-Douglas Museum, Annapolis, MD, (bottom left) Corbis, (right) D. Breitenbach/Maryland Office of Tourism Development; p. 22: (top left) P. Soran/Maryland Office of Tourism Development, (bottom left) Port Discovery, Baltimore, MD, (center right) Annie Griffiths Belt/Corbis; p. 23: (top left) D. Harp/Maryland Office of Tourism Development, (bottom right) Corbis; p. 24: AP Wide World Photos (Blake), Brown Brothers (Booth), Cinema Center Films (Holiday), North Wind Picture Archives (Hopkins); Supreme Court Historical Society (Marshall); p. 25: Major League Baseball (Ripkin), Bettmann/Corbis (Rouse), National Portrait Gallery, Smithsonian Institution (Ruth), Superstock Images (Tubman); p. 26: North Wind Picture Archives.

Photo research by Dwayne Howard

All other illustrations by John Speirs

ISBN 0-439-22285-0

THE
Jim Henson
COMPANY

12 11 10 9 8 7 6 5 4 3 2 1   1 2 3 4 5/0

Designed by Madalina Stefan

Printed in the U.S.A.

First Scholastic printing, March 2001

MARYLAND
The Old Line State

By Nancy Krulik

SCHOLASTIC INC.

New York Toronto London Auckland Sydney Mexico City New Delhi Hong Kong

A Celebration of the Fifty States

★ ★ ★ ★ ★ ★ ★ ★ ★ ★ ★ ★

In January 1999, the U.S. Mint started an ambitious ten-year program to commemorate each of the fifty United States. Over the next several years (through 2008), they will issue five newly designed quarters each year.

One side (obverse) of each new quarter will display the profile of George Washington and the words *Liberty, In God We Trust,* and *United States of America.* The other side (reverse) will feature a design honoring a specific state's unique history, the year it became a state, the year of the quarter's issue, and the words *E Pluribus Unum* (Latin for "from many, one"). The quarters are being issued in the order in which the states joined the union, beginning with the thirteen original colonies.

To find out more about the 50 State Quarters™ Program, visit the official U.S. Mint Web site at *www.usmint.gov.*

MARYLAND'S QUARTER:
The House Where History Was Made

Taking a tour through the Maryland State House is like going on a trip through U.S. history. The State House was built in 1772 and is the country's oldest state capitol building still in legislative use. The Treaty of Paris was signed by Congress there on September 3, 1783, marking the official end of the Revolutionary War. A few months later, in the same room, George Washington resigned as commander in chief of the Continental army. From November 1783 until August 1784, the Maryland State House served as the nation's first peacetime capitol.

Because the State House played such an important role in both Maryland's and the nation's history, it was chosen as the centerpiece of the Maryland quarter. The building's distinctive octagonal wooden dome (built without nails!) appears on the reverse, surrounded by leaf clusters from Maryland's state tree, the white oak. Maryland's most well-known nickname, "The Old Line State," completes the design. Maryland received this name during the Revolutionary War, in honor of its "troops of the line," soldiers from Maryland who aided General George Washington in New York in 1776 in the Battle of Long Island.

Building an Algonquin village

In the Beginning

Long before there were any settlers in the land we now call Maryland, the Chesapeake region was inhabited by Algonquian-speaking Native American tribes, which included the Choptank, Nanticoke, Patuxent, Portobago, and Wicomico. Most of the Native Americans gradually withdrew from Maryland, but their legacy remains in the names of various cities and waterways in the area. The Chesapeake Bay gets its name from Chesepiuk, an Algonquin village that once existed at the mouth of the bay. Potomac, Accokeek, and Choptank are also names of cities, towns, and rivers that are based on Native American words.

Italian explorer Giovanni da Verrazano is believed to have been the first European to have visited the area. He sailed into the Chesapeake Bay in 1524. But it was the British who eventually settled Maryland. In 1608, Captain John Smith of Virginia visited the land and wrote that there was "no place more perfect for man's habitation" than the area of land near the Chesapeake Bay.

Captain John Smith

John Smith wasn't alone in his feelings. In 1631, fur trader William Claiborne, another colonist from Virginia, opened a trading post on Kent Island in the Chesapeake Bay. Claiborne established the first European settlement in the region.

William Claiborne's trading post on Kent Island

One year later, George Calvert, the first Lord Baltimore, convinced King Charles I to grant him settlement rights to the land north of the Potomac River, which had previously been part of a grant to Virginia. Although that area included Kent Island, the king agreed to grant it to Calvert. Unfortunately, George Calvert died before the official papers could be completed. The charter for the land passed to his son Cecilius (Cecil), the second Lord Baltimore. Cecil called his new colony Maryland in honor of the king's wife, Queen Henrietta Maria.

George Calvert

In November 1633, two hundred colonists led by Cecil Calvert's younger brother, Leonard, set sail for Maryland aboard two ships, the *Ark* and the *Dove*. The settlers aboard those ships were mostly Catholics, traveling to the New World in search of religious freedom. When they reached the Maryland province in 1634, the settlers quickly purchased a Native American village and began to create a home for themselves. They named their settlement St. Mary's City.

In 1649, Maryland's population experienced a sudden jump in growth. That was the year the colonial assembly approved a law granting religious freedom to people of all faiths. Soon Puritans from Virginia flocked to Maryland as word of the state's tolerance began to spread. But the shift in the population from a Catholic majority to a Protestant majority caused problems within the colony.

Leonard Calvert and settlers with Native Americans

Laying out Baltimore, 1730

William Claiborne, unhappy about Lord Baltimore's charter to govern Maryland, claimed that Kent Island was actually part of Virginia and refused to recognize Lord Baltimore's jurisdiction over the land. In 1654, he led a group of Protestant settlers in a battle to overthrow Lord Baltimore's government. Claiborne's forces were victorious, and Claiborne was in control of Maryland for four years. In 1658, the British government demanded that he return to England, and control of the colony reverted to Lord Baltimore, a Roman Catholic.

Many of Maryland's Protestants didn't like the idea of having a Roman Catholic leader. In 1689, the newly formed Protestant Association, led by John Coode, seized control of the colonial government. John Coode demanded that England take over the leadership of the government in Maryland. King William (who became king in 1688) agreed and placed royal governors in charge of the colony.

Now that there was a new regime in power, the decision was made to move the capital from the mainly Catholic St. Mary's City to the more Protestant-populated Anne Arundel Town, which we know today as Annapolis.

In 1715, the Calvert family regained control of Maryland and retained it until the Revolutionary War.

The colony continued to grow as more towns began. In 1729, Baltimore was founded. It quickly became an important seaport and contributed to Maryland's population growth. By 1760, 162,000 people lived in the colony.

State capitol at Annapolis

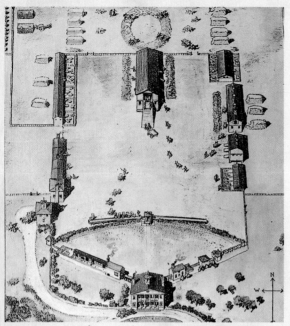
Reconstruction of an 18th-century Maryland plantation

Joining the Revolution

Patriots protesting British taxes

Maryland prospered under the Calverts' leadership. By the early 1700s, tobacco farming was bringing in big profits. Some of the colonists grew wealthy and built grand plantations. Great Britain was in debt and sought a share of the profits. England began placing huge taxes and severe trade restrictions on the colonists in order to generate revenue.

Like many other American colonists, Marylanders were infuriated by British taxation. Maryland was one of the first colonies to resist Britain's Stamp Act of 1765. The Stamp Act decreed that all printed materials — newspapers, pamphlets, official documents — had to carry a stamp that was paid for through a special tax.

Marylanders were not only quarreling with the British during the mid-1760s. They were also having disagreements with

Pennsylvanians over where the boundary should lie between their two states. Finally, land surveyors Charles Mason and Jeremiah Dixon came up with the definitive boundaries. The division between the two colonies became known as the Mason-Dixon Line. To this day, the Mason-Dixon Line is considered the border between the

Mason and Dixon

northern and the southern parts of the eastern United States.

In 1774, the British announced a new set of laws that the colonists dubbed the "Intolerable Acts," laws restricting freedom as punishment for the Boston Tea Party, a famous protest against the British tea tax that occurred in Massachusetts in November 1773. Angry Marylanders decided to have a tea party protest of their own. Soon after the new laws were imposed, the tea-carrying ship *Peggy Stewart* was burned in Annapolis harbor. That same year, delegates from Maryland attended the First Continental Congress in Philadelphia. On July 2, 1776, nearly two years after the meeting of the First Continental Congress, Maryland's delegates joined representatives from all the other colonies at the Second Continental Congress in declaring independence from Great Britain.

Although no actual battles took place on Maryland soil during the Revolutionary War, many of its men fought in battles throughout the northern colonies. During the Battle of Long Island, Maryland's soldiers helped hold the line against the British while George Washington retreated. It was from this battle that the state got its nickname, the Old Line State.

British tea on Maryland docks

In 1788, Maryland became the seventh of the newly established United States to ratify the U.S. Constitution. Three years later, Maryland agreed to give up sixty-seven square miles of land along the Potomac River for the creation of the District of Columbia, America's new national capital.

Watching the *Peggy Stewart* burn

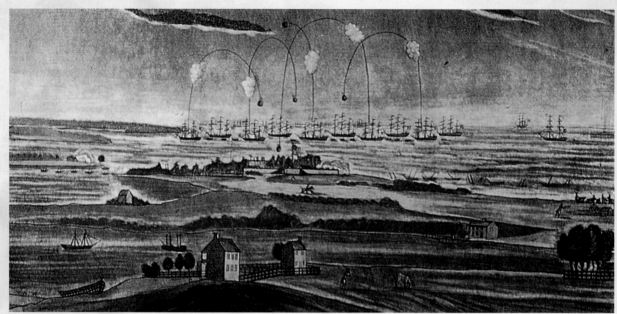

The bombardment of Fort McHenry

The War of 1812

As the nineteenth century began, there was a lot of fighting in Europe, mostly between France and England. These two nations were battling for domination — not only in Europe, but in the New World as well.

In an attempt to strengthen its military, Great Britain began seizing U.S. merchant ships and forcing the American sailors to serve in their navy. Americans resented this and, in June 1812, Congress declared war on Great Britain.

Much of the fighting of the War of 1812 took place along the Chesapeake Bay. Other battles were fought near the Canadian border and by the Gulf of Mexico. For a while, the war seemed to be going badly for the Americans. They lost many major battles, and in 1814, the British actually made their way into Washington, D.C., burning the White House and other federal buildings to the ground.

Soon after, the tide began to turn. British forces were defeated at Maryland's Fort McHenry, which guarded Baltimore's harbor, in a battle that inspired Francis Scott Key to write "The Star-Spangled Banner." Then the Americans won another major naval battle on Lake Champlain in New York. The British could see that they were not going to win the war, and they agreed to a peace treaty, which was signed by the British on December 24, 1814 and by the United States Senate on February 16, 1815.

The War of 1812 often winds up as a footnote in American history, mostly because it is sandwiched between the Revolutionary War and the Civil War. But many historians agree that it was the War of 1812 that made it clear once and for all that the United States would remain a free and independent nation, and would never again be part of Britain.

Francis Scott Key and his inspiration for "The Star-Spangled Banner"

Cover of the sheet music for the national anthem

Facts about Our National Anthem

★"The Star-Spangled Banner" was written on September 14, 1814, toward the end of the War of 1812. On September 13, 1814, a lawyer named Francis Scott Key visited the British fleet in Chesapeake Bay to help arrange for the release of an American prisoner named Dr. William Beanes. Key was able to secure the doctor's release but was forced to remain on the ship overnight because British forces had begun firing on Fort McHenry. When he awoke the next morning and saw the American flag still

flying above the fort, Key wrote a poem to commemorate the event.

★Key originally called his poem "Defense of Fort M'Henry" and wrote the original draft on the back of a letter he had in his pocket at the time.

★The melody Key chose for "The Star-Spangled Banner" was called "To Anacreon in Heaven." Nobody knows for sure who wrote the tune, but the composer is believed to be John Stafford Smith, a British musician.

★The flag that flew above Fort McHenry that fateful morning was sewn by Mary Pickersgill. It still exists and can be seen at the Smithsonian Institution's National Museum of American History in Washington, D.C.

★Although most Americans are only familiar with the first verse of our national anthem (that's the part they sing at baseball games), there are actually eight verses.

★The motto "In God We Trust," which appears on all American coins, comes from a line in the final verse of the anthem: "And this be our motto, In God We Trust."

Passengers on the Baltimore and Ohio Railroad, 1830

Links in the Chain

After the War of 1812, Maryland's residents turned their attention from war to building. They created new transportation routes — by land and by sea — and transformed Baltimore into a major industrial and trade center.

During the period between the late eighteenth and early nineteenth centuries, a series of canals were dug that connected the eastern United States to the newly developing territories in the west. Two of the canals were the Chesapeake and Ohio Canal and the Chesapeake and Delaware Canal. The new Chesapeake canals made it possible for ships to travel much faster from inland to the Atlantic Ocean by bypassing some of the inner waterways. As a result, Baltimore developed into a major U.S. seaport.

At about the same time, the first steam-powered trains were built. In 1852, work was completed on the Baltimore and Ohio Railroad, which connected the eastern states to the western settlements. The new locomotives delivered goods from the east to the west faster than ships ever could. The federal government also financed the building of a national road that started in the Maryland town of Cumberland and eventually stretched 800 miles to Vandalia, Illinois. With all these links in and out of the city, Baltimore thrived.

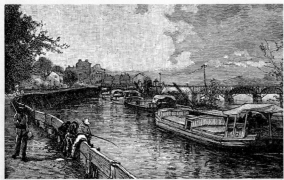
Chesapeake and Ohio Canal

Baltimore Harbor in the 1850s

Which Side Are You On?

General Jubal A. Early

As these new methods of transportation were uniting people in different areas of the country, the states themselves were becoming increasingly more divided on critical issues, especially slavery. At the time of the outbreak of the Civil War in 1861, Maryland was home to an almost equal number of free and enslaved blacks. The state's people were divided on whether or not they should side with the Union or the Confederacy in the war. However, when the neighboring state of Virginia sided with the Confederacy, Maryland suddenly became strategically important to the Union. If Maryland joined the Confederacy, Washington, D.C., would be surrounded by Confederate territories. President Lincoln quickly sent Union troops to Maryland to prevent the state from seceding. While this act may have kept Maryland from officially leaving the Union, many Marylanders left to join the Confederate forces anyway.

On September 17, 1862, General Robert E. Lee and his troops invaded Maryland. They were met by Union forces at Antietam Creek. More than 12,000 Union soldiers and 10,000 Confederates

General Robert E. Lee

Union troops at Antietam

Battle of Monocacy

were either wounded or killed during the Battle of Antietam, the bloodiest single day of fighting during the war. The Confederates soon retreated to Virginia.

In June 1863, General Lee returned to lead his troops through Maryland to Pennsylvania, where he was defeated in the Battle of Gettysburg. In July 1864, General Jubal A. Early defeated Union troops in the Battle of Monocacy, which took place near Frederick. General Early's forces were already in sight of Washington, D.C., when Union forces finally defeated them. The Battle of Monocacy marked the last attempt of the Confederacy to move north and is known as the "battle that saved Washington." The rest of the Civil War was fought in the South.

In 1864, Maryland changed its constitution. The new set of laws abolished slavery and ordered severe penalties for Marylanders who supported the Confederacy.

The Oyster Wars

Twenty-three years after the Civil War ended in 1865, Maryland found itself in a battle with its next-door neighbor, Virginia. This time the battle was over oysters. For years, fishermen in the two states had shared the right to harvest oysters in the Potomac River. But when the supply of oysters began to dwindle, Maryland's fishermen decided to impose restrictions on how much harvesting Virginia fisherman could do. The Virginians refused to agree to the new rules. Fighting broke out between the two groups of fishermen. Although a compromise was worked out in 1889, it wasn't until 1958 that a bistate commission was created to regulate the fishing industry in the Potomac River and enforce regulations.

Maryland Manufacturing

In the years following the end of the Civil War, manufacturing emerged as the mainstay of Maryland's economy. Baltimore became an international city, as immigrants from Germany, Greece, Italy, Russia, and Poland, as well as African-Americans who had migrated from more rural areas of the state, all joined together to work in Baltimore's many textile factories and shipyards. When the United States entered World War I in 1917, the demand for Maryland's industrial products grew and the state's economy boomed.

Unfortunately, Baltimore, like most industrial cities, was hit hard by the Great Depression, which struck in 1929 and lasted throughout the 1930s. During

A Maryland family during the Depression

A couple at their home in St. Mary's County, 1940

Shipbuilding in Baltimore

that dark period, Maryland passed welfare laws and approved a fifteen-million-dollar federal housing project to help ease the strain on the citizens of the state.

World War II (1939–1945) marked the end of the nation's depression, and Baltimore's factories and shipyards boomed once more, as the city provided U.S. troops with planes, ships, arms, and other military equipment. The army, navy, and air force also established military bases in Maryland, providing another boost to the state's economy.

Maryland Today

Although manufacturing has dwindled since the state's heyday during World War II, factories continue to employ Marylanders. The state's manufacturers have simply changed with the times — many companies now build computers, communication systems, and other high-tech equipment. Much of the printing for the federal government is done in Maryland as well.

Many people either commute to jobs in Washington, D.C., or work in some of the federal government's installations in Maryland, such as Andrews Air Force Base, the Goddard Space Flight Center (the flagship of NASA's

Andrews Air Force Base

space science program), and Fort Meade. The National Institutes of Health, a major federal research laboratory, is also located in Maryland.

The sea continues to pump money into Maryland's economy. For centuries, Maryland was famous for its delicious seafood (particularly Maryland blue crabs), but during the twentieth century,

Beach at Ocean City

pollution and some natural disasters upset the natural balance of chemicals in the water and greatly hurt the fishing indus-

try in the state. In 1985, major steps were taken to preserve Maryland's sea life. That year the state created the Chesapeake Cleanup Commission. The Commission is dedicated to cleaning up "toxic hot spots" caused by pollution. The effort has allowed the fish, crab, and oyster population to begin flourishing again, and industry is now on the upswing.

Tourism also provides a boost to the state's income. Year-round, visitors come to enjoy the many historical sites the state has to offer. The Appalachian Mountains in the western part of the state are popular skiing areas in the winter. During the summer, tourists flock to Maryland's beautiful beaches, such as Ocean City, a resort town on the Atlantic with a three-mile boardwalk, or the quieter spots along the Eastern Shore of the Chesapeake Bay.

In addition to the nickname "the Old Line State," Maryland is also sometimes referred to as "America in Miniature." The state acquired that title because within its 10,455 square miles, you can find mountains, forests, ocean beaches, ponds, and streams — just about any kind of natural feature (except a desert). It truly is a miniature version of our country's terrain.

Sailboats on the Chesapeake Bay

Things to Do and Places to See

Wild ponies on Assateague Island

Assateague Island National Seashore

This beautiful, unspoiled barrier island is best known for its wild ponies, which roam free within the boundaries of the island's nature preserve. They have lived on Assateague Island for centuries and are believed to be descended from small horses that swam ashore in the sixteenth century from a sinking Spanish ship.

Baltimore's bustling harbor

Baltimore's Inner Harbor

Visitors to Baltimore's Inner Harbor can ride an elevator up twenty-seven stories to the top of an observation deck for a panoramic view of the city. If traveling down below is more your style, you can take some time to explore the inside of a real World War II submarine called the *Torsk*.

The Maryland Science Center is also located in the Inner Harbor. There you can watch an IMAX film, see a show at the planetarium, or play in the science arcade, a hands-on exhibit about light, magnetism, sight, and sound.

The National Aquarium is here, too, a place where you can see sharks, sea turtles, and thousands of other fascinating creatures from under the sea. Don't forget to pay a visit to the aquarium's Marine Mammal Pavilion, where talented dolphins put on acrobatic performances.

Baltimore Civil War Museum

This museum is located right near the spot where the first fatalities of the Civil War took place. The building that houses the museum is a former train station that was a stop on the Underground Railroad. Many of the museum's exhibits pay tribute to that unique trail to freedom.

The Banneker-Douglass Museum

The Banneker-Douglass Museum

This museum is named for two great African-American Marylanders, Benjamin Banneker, a mathematician who helped survey and lay out the District of Columbia, and Frederick Douglass, a man who escaped slavery and went on to become a leader in the abolitionist movement. The museum is located in Annapolis's Mount Mariah A.M.E. Church, constructed by free blacks in 1874. Dedicated to preserving Maryland's African-American culture, the museum houses a collection of rare books, African-American art, oral histories on tape, and historical documents.

The B&O Railroad museum

The B&O Railroad Museum

The Baltimore and Ohio Railroad, the nation's first railroad to connect the Atlantic Ocean to the Ohio River, was completed in 1852. The B&O Railroad Museum celebrates the men and women who helped create it. Visitors can see actual tools used to build the railroad, as well as early railroad cars. Five buildings make up this museum, located in the Baltimore neighborhood where the B&O trains were first built in 1827.

Fort McHenry

Fort McHenry National Monument and Historic Shrine

Fort McHenry is famous as the birthplace of "The Star-Spangled Banner," but this eighteenth-century star-shaped building has served many other purposes over the years. During the Civil War, Fort McHenry was occupied by Union forces who used the fort as a prison for Confederate soldiers.

In 1933, the site became a national park. Of all the areas in the U.S. national park system, Fort McHenry is the only one designated a national monument and historical shrine.

St. Mary's City

Historic St. Mary's City

St. Mary's City in southern Maryland was the state capital of Maryland until 1695. Now a historical living museum, it still resembles a seventeenth-century city. Tour guides dressed in historically accurate clothing can show you around a replica of the first statehouse, an inn, a Native American longhouse, and a plantation. Historic St. Mary's City stretches over 800 acres.

Port Discovery

Port Discovery

Port Discovery, Baltimore's amazing children's museum, was created with the help of a team of Walt Disney Imagineers working together with educators. The museum includes a scary house filled with sensory illusions and a journey back in time to ancient Egypt, where you can find hieroglyphics and a pharoah's tomb.

The Appalachian Trail in South Mountain State Park

South Mountain State Park

South Mountain State Park in the western part of the state is only one of the forty-seven state parks that are located in Maryland. This historic park, the site of a Civil War battle in 1862 that was the staging area for the Confederate soldiers' attack at Antietam Creek a few days later, has 10,000 acres available for year-round hiking — either on foot or on cross-country skis. More than forty miles of the Appalachian Trail run along the ridge of South Mountain, with plenty of overlooks providing scenic views of the area's natural beauty. (The entire Appalachian Trail runs all the way from Georgia to Maine.)

U.S. Naval Academy

The U.S. Naval Academy

The United States Naval Academy was established in Annapolis in 1845. Today, 4,000 midshipmen call the academy's Bancroft Hall home, making it one of the largest dormitories in the world. Visitors to the Academy can view the crypt of John Paul Jones, a Scottish-born naval commander who became a commander in the Continental navy during the Revolutionary War. Many people consider him the founder of the modern navy. There's also a museum where you can see an impressive collection of model ships and exhibits about the history of the U.S. Navy.

Just Jousting

Unlike other sporting trends of the Middle Ages, jousting's popularity didn't disappear with the Knights of the Round Table. In fact, the sport's popularity grew through the ages. In the 1600s, the early colonists brought their love of jousting with them to Maryland and other colonies in the New World. The sport gained even more popularity in America during the years immediately following the Civil War.

By the 1900s, however, jousting was out of fashion with most Americans. But Marylanders were such avid jousting fans that the state legislature voted jousting Maryland's state sport in 1962.

Today, Maryland's Jousting Tournament Association holds competitions from May through October. Just as in medieval times, the competitors are called knights and ladies, and many players dress in colorful costumes. They gallop on horseback across an eighty-yard course, carrying fine-tipped lances for spearing rings. Every ring is worth points, and the competition to gather the most rings is fierce!

Famous People from Maryland

James Hubert (Eubie) Blake (1883–1983)

Baltimore-born Eubie Blake is one of the great jazz and ragtime musicians of the twentieth century. The pianist and composer wrote several early African-American musicals, including 1921's *Shuffle Along*. Some of Eubie Blake's most famous compositions include "Memories of You" and "I'm Just Wild About Harry."

John Wilkes Booth (1838–1865)

John Wilkes Booth, born near Bel Air, was already well-known as an actor when he became one of the greatest villains in American history — he's the man who assassinated Abraham Lincoln. Five days after the end of the Civil War, President Lincoln was at Ford's Theater in Washington, D.C., when Booth shot and killed him. Booth escaped and hid from the authorities for several days before being shot himself.

Billie Holiday (1915–1959)

One of the greatest jazz and blues singers of all time, Billie Holiday spent her childhood in poverty in Baltimore before moving to New York City. There she began to sing in Harlem nightclubs and became a successful recording artist. Eventually, "Lady Day" (as she was nicknamed) toured as a vocalist with some of the most famous big bands of the 1930s, 1940s, and 1950s, including the Count Basie and Artie Shaw orchestras.

Johns Hopkins (1795–1873)

Johns Hopkins, financier and philanthropist, was born on a plantation in southern Maryland. As an adult he became involved in the banking and railroad businesses and amassed a large fortune. In 1867, Hopkins founded Johns Hopkins University and Johns Hopkins Hospital. When he died, he left seven million dollars to be divided between the two institutions. Today, the hospital and university are among the finest in the nation.

Thurgood Marshall (1908–1993)

Baltimore native Thurgood Marshall was the first African-American to serve as a justice of the Supreme Court of the United States. He was appointed in 1967 by President Lyndon Johnson. Even before this civil rights leader became a justice, he'd had plenty of experience with the Supreme Court. He argued thirty-two cases before the court justices and won twenty-nine of them, including the 1954 landmark civil rights case *Brown v. Topeka Board of Education*.

Calvin (Cal) Edwin Ripkin, Jr. (1960-)

Born in the town of Havre de Grace, baseball star Cal Ripkin Jr. was signed by the Baltimore Orioles after he graduated from high school. He first played on the major league team in 1981 and soon was considered one of the best shortstops in professional baseball. Two-time winner of the American League's MVP award, Ripkin's most famous record is for consecutive games played. Between May 30, 1982 and September 6, 1995, he played in 2,131 games, breaking Lou Gehrig's record set in 1939.

James Rouse (1914–1996)

In 1995, James Rouse, real estate developer, urban planner, and native of Easton, received the Presidential Medal of Freedom. President Bill Clinton called James Rouse a hero who "helped heal the torn heart of America's cities." James Rouse started his career by building the first fully enclosed shopping malls on the East Coast. Then he turned his attention to revitalizing run-down urban areas such as Boston's famed Faneuil Hall neighborhood, the South Street Seaport in New York City, and Baltimore's Inner Harbor. All three are thriving today.

George Herman (Babe) Ruth (1895–1948)

New York's Yankee Stadium may be known as "the House that Ruth built," but it is Maryland that can take pride in the fact that the "Sultan of Swat" was a native son of Baltimore. Though many of his records have been broken over time, Babe Ruth is still one of the greatest sports legends in American history. In 1936, he was one of five original inductees into the Baseball Hall of Fame, and he was the first major sports figure to become a celebrity.

Harriet Ross Tubman (1820–1913)

Harriet Tubman was born a slave in Dorchester County. Her childhood was spent as a field hand and a house servant. In 1849, she escaped to the North with the help of a white neighbor who told her how to find the house that would be her first stop on the way to freedom. This was her introduction to the Underground Railroad, a system of helping slaves move from safe house to safe house on the road to freedom. She became very involved in the Underground Railroad movement, returning to Maryland several times to help members of her family and other slaves escape. In all, Harriet Tubman is believed to have led 300 people from slavery to freedom.

The Autobiography of Frederick Douglass

Frederick Douglass was born a slave in 1818 near Easton, Maryland. He refused to accept the fact that he would be a slave his entire life. In 1838, he escaped to Massachusetts, got married, and began a distinguished career in the abolitionist movement. He eventually went on to become an adviser to President Abraham Lincoln during the Civil War, and fought for the adoption of constitutional amendments that guaranteed voting rights and civil liberties for African-Americans.

In 1845, he completed the first version of a book called Narrative of the Life of Frederick Douglass. *Because it offered a firsthand account of the life of a slave, his book (now known as* The Autobiography of Frederick Douglass*) became an extremely valuable tool to people trying to understand the horrors of slavery during the nineteenth century.*

Frederick Douglass added to his autobiography throughout his life. He had learned at an early age that "the pathway from slavery to freedom" began with education. Below is a passage from chapter seven, describing how he learned to read and write.

My mistress was, as I have said, a kind and tenderhearted woman.... There was no sorrow or suffering for which she had not a tear. She had bread for the hungry, clothes for the naked, and comfort for every mourner that came within her reach. Slavery soon proved its ability to divest her of these heavenly qualities. Under its influence, the tender heart became stone, and the lamblike disposition gave way to one of tiger-like fierceness.

The first step in her downward course was in her ceasing to instruct me.... Nothing seemed to make her more angry than to see me with a newspaper.... She was an apt woman; and a little experience soon demonstrated, to her satisfaction, that education and slavery were incompatible with each other.

The plan which I adopted, and the one by which I was most successful, was that of making friends of all the little white boys whom I met in the street. As many of these as I could, I converted into teachers. With their kindly aid, obtained at different times and in different places, I finally succeeded in learning to read. When I was sent on errands, I always took my book with me, and by going one part of my errand quickly, I found time to get a lesson before my return.

I used also to carry bread with me, enough of which was always in the house, and to which I was always welcome; for I was much better off in this regard than many of the poor white children in our neighborhood. This bread I used to bestow upon the hungry little urchins, who, in return, would give me that more valuable bread of knowledge. . . .

The idea as to how I might learn to write was suggested to me by being in Durgin and Bailey's shipyard, and frequently seeing the ship carpenters, after hewing, and getting a piece of timber ready for use, write on the timber the name of that part of the ship for which it was intended. When a piece of timber was intended for the larboard side, it would be marked thus — "L." When a piece was for the starboard side, it would be marked thus — "S." . . . I soon learned the names of these letters, and for what they were intended when placed upon a piece of timber in the shipyard. I immediately commenced copying them, and in a short time was able to make the four letters named.

After that, when I met with any boy who I knew could write, I would tell him I could write as well as he. The next word would be, "I don't believe you. Let me see you try it." I would then make the letters which I had been so fortunate as to learn, and ask him to beat that. In this way I got a good many lessons in writing, which it is quite possible I should never have gotten in any other way.

A Snack for the Truly Crabby

Maryland blue crabs are famous the world over. Because the crabs are so abundant in the Chesapeake Bay, Marylanders have come up with thousands of ways to serve the crustaceans. Here's a simple salad that's sure to please even the crabbiest seafood lovers.

Ingredients:

One 1-pound package of elbow macaroni
Two 6-oz cans of crab meat
½ onion, chopped (ask an adult to do the chopping)
One 8-oz package of frozen peas (thawed)
1 tablespoon mayonnaise

1. Ask an adult to cook and drain the macaroni according to the directions on the package.
2. Drain the crab meat and mix in a large bowl with the macaroni, onion, and peas.
3. Mix in the mayonnaise to coat the salad.
4. Chill in the refrigerator until ready to serve.
   Makes four servings.